New Orleans: Life in an Epic City

September 11, 2001 – Hurricane Katrina, August 29, 2005

Introduced & Edited by Mary Fitzpatrick

Published by the Preservation Resource Center of New Orleans

First published in the United States of America in 2006 by

PRESERVATION RESOURCE CENTER OF NEW ORLEANS
923 Tchoupitoulas Street
New Orleans, Louisiana 70130
504/ 581-7032
www.prcno.org

C. 2006 Preservation Resource Center of New Orleans
Designer: Paula Coughlin, Typosition

Preservation Resource Center of New Orleans is a registered IRS 501 (c) (3) non-profit organization. Since 1974, the PRC's mission has been to promote the preservation, restoration and revitalization of New Orleans' historic neighborhoods and architecture.

Grateful acknowledgement is made for permission to reprint the photo of Duplain Rhodes and daughter from *The Times Picayune,* July 27, 2003, by Kathy Anderson; for permission from Louisiana State University Press to reprint a quote from *A Confederacy of Dunces,* by John Kennedy Toole, ©1980 by Thelma D. Toole; and for images copyrighted by individual photographers. Mark Sindler's photographs appear courtesy of the Louisiana Office of Tourism and the Louisiana State Museum.

Printed in China
ISBN 0-9773165-0-5

Front cover photos by R. Stephanie Bruno and Mary Fitzpatrick

Introduction

New Orleans: Life in an Epic City *is the condensed story of a particular place at a particular time. In hindsight, it is a legacy of life in New Orleans' historic neighborhoods between two American catastrophes, September 11, 2001, and Hurricane Katrina, August 29, 2005. Shortly after the first tragedy, the Preservation Resource Center of New Orleans began collecting observations and photographic images of daily life and sustaining moments in the city's 20 historic neighborhoods.*
After Katrina, many of us began digging deeper to find the essence of our beloved New Orleans.

It was in my own garden that I discovered what it means to live in this cantankerous, joyful, wounded and resilient historic city…

Special thanks to the Eugenie and Joseph Jones Family Foundation
for underwriting the publication of this book
in honor of
Stephanie Musser
Preservation Resource Center Assistant Director
1980 - 2004

My Own Sweet New Orleans

I have a garden behind a high wall in New Orleans. Through the dark alluvial soil, my banana tree creeps into the neighbor's gardenia beds, while his own confederate jasmine snakes around the rich ground and slithers up my crepe myrtle. Thick and fragrant, this shared local foliage defines our gardens.

"In New Orleans, it's impossible *not* to garden," says historian Randolph Delehanty about the fertile environment.

It's also impossible to hold back the lush culture and dense traditions that seep into the lives of anyone who calls this historic city home. Beth Ellis comes from California and soon enough she's burying her neighbor's St. Joseph statue under the flowers for good luck in the local real estate market. Iain Baird moves to New Orleans from

Washington, D.C., and decorates a room in his new house with purple, green and gold Mardi Gras beads.

Maybe some people think they can just live here and the native ways won't mushroom into their own private patch, but mostly we're enveloped in the richness. Eventually, the eccentricities and the sense of such a place are passed along to us, and from the abundance we cultivate our own sweet New Orleans.

© RICHARD SEXTON

© David Spielman

"Warm nests in old haunts," author Mimi Read calls the ripened places and traditions that New Orleanians love and nurture.

Cherished rituals and beloved corners of the city belong to us all: Orleans Avenue when the Endymion Parade rolls past, the bandstand at Audubon Park, a scrambled egg po-boy at Elizabeth's, a domino match on the LaSalle Street neutral ground, Pirate's Alley in the fog, reading the *Times Picayune* obituaries while drinking coffee and chicory on a Garden District gallery, second line parading in Tremé, a worn bar stool at Parasol's, or whitewashing the family tomb on All Saints Day.

The culture creeps into our lives with the pungency of a sweet olive tree on a balmy night. One day you're riding the streetcar to work and the elderly lady who gets on at Jackson Avenue passes king

cake slices to everyone on board. You get the baby hidden inside, so the next week you bring the king cake. Now, when faraway friends ask, you no longer say that you love New Orleans but can't exactly explain where her charm lies. You tell them what happens on the streetcar every Friday morning from Twelfth Night to Mardi Gras and that whoever bites into the plastic baby in the king cake has to bring a cake for everyone else the

MARY FITZPATRICK

next week. That's your New Orleans.

There are nearly a half million people who call this town home, and in each life there is a tradition, a neighborhood, a street, a house, an inherited ritual, some mundane experience, or exotic person or colloquialism that defines their city, setting it apart from anywhere else on the planet.

"It's the wild parrots in the palm at Camp and Felicity and the framing of

RAYMOND YOUNG

St. Mary's domed steeple between the rectangles of the towers of St. Alphonsus," says Camille Strachan. "It's the steamboat houses from the levee, the skyline viewed from Bayou St. John. It's a carnival ball from the balcony and the free the-ater in City Council cham-bers."

"It's driving past Mardi Gras World on the way to work and yielding to a fork lift bearing a giant gorilla head across the road," says

Dale Irvin, "a place and a moment that could only exist in New Orleans."

And so the culture grows on us. The rich

soil becomes firm ground and just like the rooted natives, newcomers cannot leave.

One-time Chicago cop Tony Carter was seduced by the city even before he got here. After watching Richard Gere drag a sultry Kim Bassinger out of the Possum Lounge in Algiers Point, he came to

BRYON CORNELISON

New Orleans in search of the bar featured in the 1986 thriller *No Mercy.*

"I found out it didn't exist," Tony says, "but I fell in love with the rundown beautiful houses in the neighborhood, moved to the Point with a pot bellied pig, bought a bar, began renovating buildings, married a girl from Iowa who walked into my bar one night in 1994, and celebrated ten years in Algiers Point with an alligator

and sausage gumbo feast. This is it, this is home."

A self-described fifth-generation French Quarter rat, James Nolan left for three decades until baited back by a rose-colored courtyard on Dauphine Street. Nancy Tervalon King returned to Tremé after 40 years in Houston because she missed her 54 first cousins and 101 cousins once-removed on her

MARY FITZPATRICK

mother's side.

"The main reason people like me cannot truly leave New Orleans," writes Mimi Read in her essay "The Trying-to-Leave-New Orleans Blues," "is that in growing up here, we absorb such a potent and irrefutable sense of place that the rest of America will always seem insipid by comparison. We can't leave. Where would we go?"

Where could we experience such diverse cultures planted so tightly together? Where could we wake up to the Original Prince of Wales Social Aid and Pleasure Club parading down the street in lime green suits on an ordinary Sunday? Where else in America would Twelfth Night incite a city to erupt in plumage and mystic celebration that culminates weeks later with ashes on our foreheads? Where else could you have a name like Hypolite Begue or Parfait Dupuy and live in the modern-day

medieval bazaar that old timers call The Quarters? Where else would your father teach you to drive in the cemetery while giving a tutorial on the families buried in each tomb?

I sit in my garden at dusk, watching the sun set through the thick branches of live oak trees. The roots of the trees, planted many generations ago, crowd the bricks of the courtyard, laid by men long dead. I crush a leaf from the ginger in my hand and breathe in the spicy scent. An acquaintance from Bywater on the other side of town gave me the bulb for this plant. Now it spreads profusely from my garden to my neighbor's. I have dug up these bulbs and shared them with friends across the river. Up from the earth, down through generations, across neighborhoods and over the Mississippi River, this lush piece of life radiates in every direction.

MARY FITZPATRICK

KATHERINE LAWSON HART

My garden is my own sweet New Orleans, but like the abundant traditions and bountiful culture of this city, it swells into the street and across town.

Mary Fitzpatrick, December 2005
Preservation Resource Center of New Orleans
mfitzpatrick@prcno.org

New Orleans: Life in an Epic City

September 11, 2001 – Hurricane Katrina, August 29, 2005

Introduced & Edited by Mary Fitzpatrick

Published by the Preservation Resource Center of New Orleans

GENTILLY TERRACE

SOUTH LAKEVIEW

CITY PARK

METAIRIE ROAD

CITY PARK AVENUE

PARKVIEW

ESPLANADE RIDGE

NEW MARIGNY

ORLEANS

CANAL

SOUTH BROAD

AIRLINE DRIVE

MID-CITY

TREMÉ

FRENCH QUARTER

FAUBOURG MARIGNY

BYWATER

HOLY CROSS

TULANE

EARHART EXPRESSWAY

CENTRAL BUSINESS DISTRICT

ALGIERS POINT

BROADMOOR

CLAIBORNE

CARROLLTON

CENTRAL CITY

LOWER GARDEN DISTRICT

NAPOLEON

UPTOWN

GARDEN DISTRICT

ST. CHARLES

AUDUBON PARK

MAGAZINE

IRISH CHANNEL

TCHOUPITOULAS

MISSISSIPPI RIVER

WEST BANK

New OrLeans
Neighborhoods in
National Register of Historic Places

Y ou can go into any neighborhood and find all of New Orleans.

James Sallis
Writer

Neighborhoods in National Register of Historic Places, by Paula Coughlin
French Quarter, © Richard Sexton
Magazine Street, Lower Garden District, by Mary Fitzpatrick
Faubourg Marigny, by Mark Sindler

T he nature of New Orleans is
to encourage the optimum
development of New Orleanians:
it's an environment
for a specific form of life.

Andrei Codrescu
National Public Radio Poet on Call

Faubourg Marigny, by Akbar Nimji
Audubon Park, Uptown, by René Guitart
Zulu election day, Tremé, by Mary Fitzpatrick
Seersucker suit & white bucks, Central Business District, by Mary Fitzpatrick
Mardi Gras bead skirts and Zulu coconuts, by Alysha Jordan

N ew Orleans has a body and a soul.
The soul is the people,
and the body is the historic architecture.

Camille Strachan
Attorney

Garden District, by Mary Fitzpatrick
Mid-City, by Ian McNulty
Dancing Zydeco, French Quarter, by Mark Sindler

Growing up in New Orleans
teaches you to relish diversity.
Just as jazz and jambalaya get their
flavors from many ingredients,
in New Orleans you learn that a good
life includes appreciating all types of
people and styles and attitudes.

Walter Isaacson
C.E.O., Aspen Institute
Vice Chairman, Louisiana Recovery Authority

Barkus Parade, French Quarter, by Mary Fitzpatrick
Zulu Parade, Central City, by Robert Wolf
Super Sunday Mardi Gras Indians, Mid-City, by Mark Sindler
St. Patrick's Day, Irish Channel, by Melanie Miranda
St. Joseph's Day Parade, French Quarter, by Todd Price

Anything could happen there, in the blocks of houses too beautiful to be true.

Oliver La Farge 1901-1963
Anthropologist

French Quarter, by Mark Sindler
Esplanade Ridge, by Mary Fitzpaatrick
Tremé, by Mary Fitzpatrick
Uptown, by Michelle Kimball
Steamboat House, Lower Ninth Ward–Holy Cross, by Tolton Connor Jr.
Julia Row, Central Business District, by Meg Lousteau
Faubourg Marigny, by Mary Fitzpatrick
African-American Museum of Art, Culture & History, Tremé, by Naydja Bynum
French Quarter, by Mary Fitzpatrick
Garden District, © Frank Relle

Dad taught me to drive in the cemetery. "Proceed slowly past the Westfeldts, come to a complete stop at the Dugans, now back up in a straight line to the Fitzpatricks."

Fletcher Dugan Westfeldt Fitzpatrick
Senate staffer

Faubourg New Marigny, © Richard Sexton
Esplanade Ridge, © Mason Florence
Faubourg New Marigny, by Tracey Hogan

W hether I'm in Cochin, India
or Golden Meadow, Louisiana, having
a passport from New Orleans always
assures me undivided attention.
The Governor of Mumbai
didn't bat an eye at my best friend
from New York but when he found out
I was from New Orleans,
he looked on me like a
rare and perfumed species.

Angele Parlange
Stylist, designer, author

Garden District, by Mary Fitzpatrick
French Quarter, by Mark Sindler

When my cousin's dog Tequila ran away

I knew he was cruising around

those sassy Garden District

poodles Martini and Cognac.

Sure enough, they were having a

big time in the garden of

Our Lady of Perpetual Help

over on Prytania Street.

Lisa Langhoff
Attorney

Tremé, by Amy Loewy
Saturn Parade, Central Business District, by Kevin Kelly
French Quarter, by Wendi Berman
French Quarter, © David Dillard
Barkus Parade, French Quarter, by Mary Fitzpatrick
French Quarter, by Robert Holland

GRIS GRIS
TAROT CARDS
SPIRITUAL ADVISOR
HERBS
ROOTS
READINGS

In London they say
if two people stand on a corner,
a queue forms.
In New Orleans, a parade starts.

Marda Burton
Writer

Satchmo Summerfest, Tremé, by Mark Sindler
Miss Junior Achievement at Barkus Parade, French Quarter, by Mary Fitzpatrick
Rex Parade, Garden District, by Nairne Frazar
Masons parading out of Armstrong Park, Tremé, by Keith Weldon Medley
"Antoine's on the West Bank," Algiers Point, by Bryon Cornelison
Super Sunday stilt walker, Mid-City, by Mark Sindler

I liked it all from the first:
I lingered long in that morning
walk, liking it more and
more, in spite of its shabbiness,
but utterly unable to
say then or ever since
wherein its charm lies.

Charles Dudley Warren
1829-1900
Newspaperman

Algiers Point, by Tony Carter
Carrollton, by Mary Fitzpatrick
French Quarter, by Michelle Kimball

Being Catholic in New Orleans means there's no real separation between daily life, spiritual life and an excuse for a good party. The city happily travels on a pilgrimage through the liturgical year – Mardi Gras, Ash Wednesday, Lent, St. Patrick's Day, Palm Sunday, Easter, All Saint's Day. And we meander along the journey. Thanksgiving Mass at Our Lady of Prompt Succor to thank Mary for saving the city at the Battle of New Orleans. Fig cookies on a St. Joseph Altar to thank him for rescuing us from famine. Votives to St. Roch for his help in curing broken hearts and limbs. We live our faith in many ways. Mostly we celebrate it.

Deb McDonald
Bookseller

St. Joseph's Altar, Garden District, by Mary Fitzpatrick
St. Joseph's Day Parade, French Quarter, by Todd Price
Faubourg New Marigny, by Tolton Connor Jr.
Votive offerings to St. Roch, Faubourg New Marigny, by Averil Oberhelman
King of Carnival, Garden District, by Nairne Frazar

I fear for the children: innocent victims of Subway sandwiches who might never know the crunch of French bread and fried oysters.

Sandy Whann
President, Leidenheimer Bakery

Irish Channel and French Quarter, by Mark Sindler

I t's not what you wore or the parties that you remember forever. It's the tradition. The fact that my grandmother helped me with every little detail just as she helped my mom when she made her debut—that's what made being a deb so special.

Joy Rovaris
Queen, Original Illinois Club Ball, 2005

Amanda Duplynn Rhodes, Queen for the 2003 Young Men Illinois Ball, and her father, Duplain Rhodes III, by Kathy Anderson,

Shelby Scott Westfeldt, 2003 Queen of Carnival,
with her father, Thomas D. Westfeldt II, by Mary Fitzpatrick

It's all about family.

Nina Walmsley
Queen, Mistick Krewe of Comus, 2005

There is no, no, no, no place
like New Orleans for music.
The pioneers are here.
We built the house.
You can redecorate it,
but we laid the foundation.

Dave Bartholomew
Trumpeter

French Quarter, by Mark Sindler
Aaron Neville at Jazz Fest, near Esplanade Ridge, by Mark Sindler
Mississippi Riverbank, French Quarter, © David Dillard

W hen I find myself slipping into
a not-so-great mood, I think back to
my rides home from high school.
There's this bend in St. Charles
Avenue where the sun pours down at
the end of the day and the trees make
the light dance on the street.
In my mind now I can feel the wind
with my windows rolled down, and
it just makes me so happy again.

Ainsley Hines
Graduate student

St. Charles Avenue, Garden District, by Cheryl Gerber
St. Charles Avenue, Uptown, by Mary Fitzpatrick
Garden District, by Michelle Kimball

Follow the formica…that's my advice. Tablecloths and maitre d's are fine for the other guy, but give me fried oysters, chipped countertops, and a husky voiced waitress who calls me "baby" and throws in a little lagniappe. Serve me up a po-boy dressed, and then just let me die right there, head down on the formica, and I won't have any regrets.

Anthony Probst
Construction

Johnny's, French Quarter, by Mark Sindler
Katie's Restaurant, Mid-City, by Mary Fitzpatrick
Atchafalaya Café, Irish Channel, by Mary Fitzpatrick

French Quarter, by Mark Sindler
French Quarter, by Cheryl Gerber
St. Roch Chapel, Faubourg New Marigny, by Averil Oberhelman
French Quarter, by Mary Fitzpatrick

I come from a long line of Quarter rats. We inhabit crumbling buildings, seldom poke our snouts out of the French Quarter, and like our distant cousins the cockroaches, can stay up all night and will eat anything.

James Nolan
Writer

I find solace in the river. I moved to a house near the levee in Algiers Point, and most mornings I take the ferry to my studio in Marigny. Crossing the river is a ritual for me. It's symbolic, like the short trip across Istanbul's Bosphorus Straits that takes you from Europe to Asia. I make a trek from the western to the eastern United States daily. "Going to town" as the old-line Algerines under-describe it.

Richard Sexton
Photographer, writer

Crossing the Mississippi from Algiers Point toward the French Quarter, by Cheryl Gerber
From the French Quarter toward Algiers Point, © 2005 Neil Alexander

First bite, Garden District, by Beverly Lamb
Hubig's Pies factory, Faubourg Marigny, by Mary Fitzpatrick

I knew I wasn't in Maine anymore when I started buying the cash register snacks at my corner store: Zapp's spicy Cajun crawtator chips, LeJeune's ginger cake, Praline Ring candied pecans, and those teeny dried shrimp. But my most favorite of all is Hubig's coconut cream pie. I could talk about that pie forever.

Erika Marks Brauner
Illustrator

Galatoire's, French Quarter, © 2005 Louis Sahuc
Galatoire's waiter John Fontenot, by Cheryl Gerber

Ducking out of the heat and traffic of Bourbon Street and into the cool interior of Galatoire's is an experience as near to time travel as one can find these days.

Arthur Nead
New Orleans writer

W hen I was coming up, everyone sat
outside in the evenings, and music was everywhere.
The Dixie Cups and later the Neville Brothers
got started right there. As kids we would grab
boxes or cans or whatever we could find to
beat on and jam with. By nine I was arranging
music and by fourteen I was performing gospel,
rhythm and blues and jazz in nightclubs.
How could I grow up to do anything else?

Henry Butler
Pianist

The Andrews Family, Tremé, by Cheryl Gerber
Uptown, by Mary Fitzpatrick
Jazzman Kid Ory's former home, Central City, © Neil Alexander
Esplanade Ridge, by Raymond Young

"**I** shall have a cup,"
Ignatius said grandly.
"Chicory coffee with boiled milk."
"Only instant," the bartender replied.
"I can't possibly drink that," Ignatius
told his mother.
"It's an abomination."

John Kennedy Toole
Confederacy of Dunces

The cupper (coffee taster), Central Business District, by Bryan Fitzpatrick
Café du Monde, French Quarter, by Mark Sindler

Dr. Bob in front of his Airstream, Bywater, by Julie McCollam
Bywater, by Mary Fitzpatrick

A really great day in Bywater?
We start mid-morning at Elizabeth's for a spicy sausage po-boy and praline bacon, then take in a couple of stoop sales on Dauphine and wander over to the Bywater Art Market on Piety to look at Dr. Bob's latest creations. After a nap, we open the shutters and take the dogs for a sunset walk on the Industrial Canal levee. Then it's back home for an impromptu crawfish boil and cocktails in the courtyard with a few friends, listening to the sounds of live jazz and the river float over the rooftops.

Daniel McElmurray
Landscape architect

W hat's worth doing in
New Orleans is worth overdoing.

Becky Allen
Entertainer

Bead tree, Uptown, by Robert Holland
French Quarter, by Robert Holland

Sometimes I begin with a minor character and the character takes shape in my head, and I realize that that person couldn't possibly exist anywhere except New Orleans.

Julie Smith
Mystery writer

French Quarter, by Mark Sindler
Carrollton, by Mary Fitzpatrick

People here loved to have
fun when they drank. They filled
the bars and toasted each other across
the tables and nattered about
the Saints, politics, what they
had eaten for lunch, what they were
going to eat for dinner.

Poppy Z. Brite
Author

Ladies in Red gala, Central Business District, by Jim Thorns
Men in white linen at Antoine's, French Quarter, by Tave Fitzpatrick
Leah Chase, Tremé, © David Spielman

You know
New Orleans is home
hen you think the colors
purple, green, and gold
look good together.

Anonymous

g Marigny, by Mary Fitzpatrick
Parade, Armstrong Park, Tremé, by Deb McDonald
by Mary Fitzpatrick

New Orleans, unlike most of America, is not a melting pot. It's a gumbo, where all the ingredients add to the mix but keep their distinctive flavor at the same time.

Roberts Batson
Humorist, actor, writer, tour guide

French Quarter, by Mark Sindler
Crescent City Farmers Market, © Richard McCarthy
Dillard University, Gentilly, by Mary Fitzpatrick
Saving Coliseum Square in 1970s, photographer unknown
Domilise's, Uptown, by Mary Fitzpatrick
Frenchmen Street, Faubourg Marigny, by Averil Oberhelman
St. Charles Streetcar, © Richard Sexton
Barkus Parade ladder, French Quarter, by Mary Fitzpatrick
Checkers, Tremé, © Christopher Porché West
White Linen Night, Central Business District, by Mark Sindler

New Orleans has become one of the cities of the mind and is therefore immortal.

Cleanth Brooks 1906-1994
Literary critic

Orpheus Parade passing Gallier Hall, 2003, Central Business District, by Mark Sindler
St. Roch Cemetery, Faubourg New Marigny, by Sara Orton
Holy Cross levee, by Mary Fitzpatrick

St. Roch Cemetery, Faubourg New Marigny, © Mason Florence
Rampart Street, Tremé, by Mark Sindler

Ⅰn New Orleans you dream. You suffer.
Then you celebrate. It's a strange and
unusual place, and it makes you strange
and unusual if you're from there or live
there. It's always a great advantage to be
strange and unusual. It's been the ace in
my back pocket—New Orleans.
It's a mark of distinction.

Nancy Lemann
Author

Leaving New Orleans is like finishing
a very long, very good book.
But suddenly, something's missing.
A part of you is left in the last chapter.
You want to jump back into the pages as if
you were never there and do it all again.

Nick Marinello
New Orleans writer

Faulkner House Books, French Quarter, © Richard Sexton
Audubon Park, Uptown, by Mark Sindler

The feelings get stronger
the longer I stay away.
The more that I miss New Orleans.

Louis Armstrong   1901-1971
Jazzman

City Park Carousel, by Mark Sindler
French Quarter, by Mary Fitzpatrick

DEDICATED TO THE COURAGEOUS CITIZENS OF NEW ORLEANS WHO ARE RESTORING THEIR HOMES, BUSINESSES, NEIGHBORHOODS AND LIVES AFTER THE TRAGEDY OF HURRICANE KATRINA.

South Lakeview, by Cheryl Gerber
Bywater, by Mary Fitzpatrick
Mid-City, by Mark Sindler

THE PRESERVATION RESOURCE CENTER OF NEW ORLEANS
THANKS THE PROFESSIONAL AND AMATEUR PHOTOGRAPHERS WHO
DONATED THE USE OF THEIR IMAGES FOR THIS BOOK.

NEIL ALEXANDER	RENE GUITART	KEITH WELDON MEDLEY
WENDI BERMAN	KATHERINE LAWSON HART	MELANIE MIRANDA
R. STEPHANIE BRUNO	TRACEY HOGAN	AKBAR NIMJI
NAYDJA BYNUM	ROBERT HOLLAND	AVERIL OBERHELMAN
TONY CARTER	ALYSHA JORDAN	SARA ORTON
TOLTON CONNOR, JR.	KEVIN KELLY	CHRISTOPHER PORCHÉ WEST
BRYON CORNELISON	MICHELLE KIMBALL	TODD PRICE
DAVID DILLARD	BEVERLY LAMB	FRANK RELLE
BRYAN FITZPATRICK	MEG LOUSTEAU	LOUIS SAHUC
MARY FITZPATRICK	AMY LOEWY	RICHARD SEXTON
TAVE FITZPATRICK	RICHARD MCCARTHY	DAVID SPIELMAN
MASON FLORENCE	DEB McDONALD	MARK SINDLER
ROBERT FLORENCE	JULIE MCCOLLAM	JIM THORNS
NAIRNE FRAZAR	IAN MCNULTY	ROBERT WOLF
CHERYL GERBER		RAYMOND YOUNG